FANTASY TEAM
95/96
THE REVENGE

This book is dedicated to
Richard's sisters Jo and Erica;
and to Jason's nan and granddad
Lily and Len Agombar.

FANTASY TEAM 95/96

THE REVENGE

JASON PAGE and RICHARD MEAD
ILLUSTRATIONS BY DAVID WOODWARD

BLOOMSBURY

The publishers would like to thank Ches Stich for her help.

First published in Great Britain in 1995 by
Bloomsbury Children's Books, 2 Soho Square, London W1V 5DE.

A CIP catalogue record for this book is available from the
British Library.

ISBN 0-7475-2250-2

10 9 8 7 6 5 4 3 2 1

Printed in Great Britain by Cox and Wyman, Reading.

Chapter One

HERE WE GO

HERE WE GO, HERE WE GO (AGAIN!)

It's back. And it's better than ever! Yes, *Fantasy Team*, the soccer sensation that swept the nation returns for a new season of footie fun. It's fast and it's furious. In fact it's fuming mad.

It's the game which turns YOU into the manager of your very own football club. You get to chose **real** soccer stars who play in **real** matches. We're giving you £25 million to select a dream team of your favourite players. Don't expect an easy ride though. Soon you'll be joining the Premiership and pitching your side against the best teams in the land.

But we're angry. Why? Well, last season the team **we** picked to explain the rules to **you** got marmalised, ending up a miserable 14th in the Premiership. Beaten at our own game – oh, the humiliation! To make things worse, while we were floundering around in the relegation zone, loads of *Fantasy Team* managers wrote in, telling us their sides were battling with Blackburn right up at the top of the League table. Thanks for that!

Now we've got the chance to level the score in a new version of the game. Don't worry if you haven't played *Fantasy Team* before. You'll soon pick up the rules. And for all you veteran *Fantasy Team* managers from last season we've introduced lots of exciting new features – including loads of Jeff the Ref bonus points.

And speaking of Jeff, let's introduce him! Jeff the Ref is *Fantasy Team*'s radical referee. As well as ensuring fair play he's always on hand to give advice and tips on playing the game. And wise words aren't the only thing Jeff dishes out. He can also award extra points to hard-working managers.

Before we get into all of that, however, let's have a look at what's in store for you in the rest of the book!

⊛ **Chapter Two, Selecting Your Star Squad**: The first thing you do as a *Fantasy Team* manager is select your squad of players. Every single soccer star in the Premiership is up for grabs – at a price! Even with £25 million you'll have to budget carefully.

⊛ **Chapter Three, How You Score**: Once you've picked your side it's time to discover how they earn you points. The scoring system is easy to understand. It all depends on how the players you've selected perform in **real** football games!

⊛ **Chapter Four, Race For The Premiership**: Now you're ready to join the Premiership. It's the ultimate test of your team – and your skill as manager. Prepare to take on all the top teams as you battle for position on the league table.

⊛ **Chapter Five, Making Transfers**: You hired them – and you can fire them! As the season progresses you may want to sell some of your old players and buy new talent. This chapter on transfers explains all.

You can start playing *Fantasy Team* any time you like.

Don't worry if the football season is already under way. You can easily catch up any weeks you've missed – just check out the **Late Kick-off** questions at the back of the book. And remember you can play *Fantasy Team* on your own or against your friends. All your pals can join in with rival teams – but if they don't have their own copy of the book they'll have to make copies of the Score Charts for themselves.

Which leaves just one more thing to say –

GOOD LUCK!

Chapter Two

SELECTING YOUR STAR SQUAD

OK – so maybe our dream team last year wasn't quite the champion side we'd hoped for. But do you think you could do any better? Well, here's your chance to find out. It's time to pick your players and head off for the Premiership!

SHOP TILL YOU DROP!

It's time to go shopping. Don't worry, we're not sending you off to BHS with your Mum for those lime green slacks she thinks are perfect for you. Nope, you're about to buy eleven top talented footballers – and it's not going to cost you a penny!

YOU'RE IN THE MONEY!

We're giving you £25,000,000 to spend. That's just like winning the National Lottery three weeks in a row! Or being Queen for a day (and you won't even have to feed the corgis!).

Unfortunately, you're not going to be Richie Rich for long. You'll need all that money for buying players, and top footballers don't come cheap – just ask Alex Ferguson! If you splash out on Shearers, Suttons and Schmeichels, you'll end up with a six-man squad!

HOW TO PICK YOUR TEAM

Fantasy teams have the same formation as your favourite Premiership side. Your squad will include one goalkeeper, four defenders and six forwards. You can use any combination of full backs and centre backs for your defenders. Forwards can be chosen from midfielders and strikers. And that dodgy looking bloke who stands at the back of the field wearing a horrible shirt – that's your goalie, that is!

Don't worry about substitutes – you can't have any! The eleven players you're about to pick will play for you every week. It's no problem if one of them is injured or ends up helping the police with their enquiries! As the season continues you can transfer players in and out of your team – Chapter Five tells

you all about this. But for now, you just need to
think about those eleven players who will make up
your *Fantasy Team*.

THE NAME GAME

Now it's time for the team selection. Any footballer
currently playing in the FA Premiership is up for
selection. To help you choose, we've listed, the good,
the bad and the Vinnys. Can you pick a League-
winning side or is there a place in the GM Vauxhall
Conference waiting for you?

THE DECISION IS YOURS!

There are three categories of players. First up are the
Fantasy Fantastics – a super squad of star strikers
and dazzling defenders *(see page 14)*. They'd make an
unbeatable team, if only you could afford them! You
can splash out on one or two, but leave enough cash
for the rest of your players!

You'll probably get most of your side from the **Premier Premiership Players** *(see page 17)*. All the Premiership sides are listed team by team and six players have been selected from each. It's a mixture of footballing faves and new names. You'll need all your soccer know-how to separate the future Bobby Moores from the Bobby not-quite-as-Muchs!

If you're planning to change your name to Kenny Dalglish and pick the whole of Blackburn Rovers, I've got some bad news! You can only have a maximum of three players from any one club.

Last, and probably least, we have the **Bargain Basement** *(see page 24)*. Here you can choose any player we haven't already listed. The price you pay depends on the club they play for. Simple, isn't it?

If you're playing *Fantasy Team* against a friend, take turns choosing your squad. If you both want the same player, then hold an auction. The person who bids the most money wins!

PENALTY POWERHOUSE

When you've selected your squad, you'll need to

choose two players to take the penalties. These should be the two players in your *Fantasy Team* who you think will score the most goals for your team. You'll find out in Chapter Four how they can score extra League points for your side. Put a star on your Score Charts next to the two players who you expect to score the most goals.

DON'T BE A FOOL – REMEMBER THE RULES

Now you're ready to spend, spend, spend – but never forget the three golden rules.

1. Your squad must have one goalkeeper, four defenders and six forwards.

2. You must not spend more than £25 million.

3. You must not choose more than three players from any one Premiership side.

✪ THE FANTASY FANTASTICS ✪

Our Heavenly Eleven League Leaders

GOALKEEPER

✪ **Tim Flowers £4 million**
Blackburn Rovers

It's no good spending all your money on goal-scorers if you can't keep the ball out of your own net. Here's the answer! Flowers has guarded the goal for Southampton, Blackburn and England – will he do the same for you?

DEFENDERS

✪ **Stig Bjornebye £3.6 million**
Liverpool

The Nineties Reds are starting to look more like the awesome side of the Eighties, with a back four that could stop an avalanche. With some impressive play last season, we reckon this will be the Norwegian's year.

✪ **Andy Hinchcliffe £3.5 million**
Everton

Everton had a patchy season last year. But their brilliant victory in the FA Cup showed them at their best. Hinchcliffe not only brilliantly blocks goals for Everton - his demon left foot sets up plenty as well!

⊛ Tony Adams £4.1 million
Arsenal

Adams has played over 300 games for Arsenal. Under his captaincy, they've won the FA Cup, the League Cup and come top of the First Division. A superb centre back, he could pick up a lot of points for your team.

⊛ Darren Peacock £3.8 million
Newcastle United

The Magpies know a good thing when they see it. They paid QPR £2.7 million – a club record – for Peacock, and it's been money well spent. With players like Peacock, no wonder Newcastle supporters can say, "Andy who?".

FORWARDS

⊛ Ryan Giggs £4.5 million
Manchester United

At the start of last season, critics were saying that Giggs was burnt out – and he wasn't even 21! In 1995 we saw him back at his best. The Welsh wizard could work magic for your team!

⊛ Darren Anderton £4.1 million
Tottenham Hotspur

Spurs began the 1994-95 season looking like they were heading for Division 1. But Anderton's perfect placing of the ball had them zooming upwards instead. An England regular – and goal scorer against Greece – Anderton is one to watch.

⚽ Chris Bart-Williams £4.0 million
Sheffield Wednesday

Do the Bart-man and you could be doing yourself a
big favour. This 21-year-old midfield marvel is one of
the brightest stars in the Premiership. His blistering
goal against Liverpool last season was perfect proof of
this.

⚽ Gary Speed £3.8 million
Leeds United

Speed has been at Elland Road for the whole of his
career, and you can see why they don't want to let
him go! A midfield player with a great scoring record,
he could have your team speeding up the League
table!

⚽ Alan Shearer £4.5 million
Blackburn Rovers

Words fail us! In 1993-94 Shearer scored almost half
the Rovers' League goals. Last season he was the
leading goal-scorer in the Premiership. Just imagine
how many he might get this season – and they could
be for your team!

⚽ Andy Cole £4.5 million
Manchester United

Alex Ferguson may think Andy's worth £7 million
but you can buy him for two-thirds of the price with
Fantasy Team! Cole has really settled in at Old
Trafford – his five goals against Ipswich proved that in
spectacular style!

THE PREMIER
✪ PREMIERSHIP PLAYERS ✪

A super six-shooter from every Premiership side

✪ Arsenal
Will the Highbury boys become high-flyers again?

Goalie	Seaman	£2.8 million
Defender	Dixon	£2.7 million
Defender	Winterburn	£2.2 million
Forward	Wright	£3.2 million
Forward	Hartson	£2.5 million
Forward	Merson	£2.1 million

✪ Aston Villa
With prices like these the Villans are a steal!

Goalie	Bosnich	£0.9 million
Defender	Ehiogu	£0.7 million
Defender	Staunton	£1.0 million
Forward	Yorke	£1.2 million
Forward	Saunders	£0.9 million
Forward	Townsend	£0.7 million

✪ Blackburn Rovers
Kenny's lads are hoping for more of the same.

Goalie	Mimms	£2.3 million
Defender	Le Saux	£3.8 million
Defender	Berg	£3.5 million
Forward	Sherwood	£3.6 million
Forward	Sutton	£4.0 million
Forward	Ripley	£3.3 million

✪ Bolton Wanderers
Wandering up the Premiership.

Goalie	Branagan	£1.7 million
Defender	Phillips	£1.6 million
Defender	Stubbs	£1.9 million
Forward	McAteer	£1.9 million
Forward	McGinlay	£1.7 million
Forward	Patterson	£1.5 million

✪ Chelsea
Will you make a Wise move with the Blues?

Goalie	Kharine	£2.5 million
Defender	Sinclair	£2.2 million
Defender	Johnsen	£2.4 million
Forward	Stein	£2.9 million
Forward	Wise	£2.7 million
Forward	Peacock, G.	£2.5 million

✪ Coventry City
A great place to be sent after all!

Goalie	Ogrizovic	£1.1 million
Defender	Pickering	£0.9 million
Defender	Borrows	£1.3 million
Forward	Wegerle	£0.8 million
Forward	Ndlovu	£1.2 million
Forward	Dublin	£1.6 million

✪ Everton
Goodison Park – a good place to start!

Goalie	Southall	£1.5 million
Defender	Ablett	£1.6 million

Defender	Watson	£1.3 million
Forward	Rideout	£1.8 million
Forward	Amokachi	£1.6 million
Forward	Limpar	£1.5 million

⊛ Leeds United
Will they be Leeding from the front?

Goalie	Lukic	£2.9 million
Defender	Dorigo	£2.8 million
Defender	Kelly	£3.1 million
Forward	Yeboah	£3.5 million
Forward	Deane	£2.9 million
Forward	McAllister	£3.2 million

⊛ Liverpool
Dive into the 'pool.

Goalie	James	£3.1 million
Defender	Babb	£3.3 million
Defender	Scales	£3.0 million
Forward	Fowler	£3.8 million
Forward	Rush	£3.2 million
Forward	Barnes	£3.0 million

⊛ Manchester City
Will you Coton on to the bargains here?

Goalie	Coton	£0.7 million
Defender	Curle	£1.0 million
Defender	Flitcroft	£0.8 million
Forward	Quinn	£0.9 million
Forward	Rosler	£1.4 million
Forward	Walsh	£1.0 million

⊛Manchester United
Can they make it back to the top?

Goalie	Schmeichel	£3.7 million
Defender	Bruce	£3.2 million
Defender	Irwin	£3.5 million
Forward	Hughes	£3.6 million
Forward	Ince	£3.3 million
Forward	Cantona	£3.0 million

⊛Middlesborough
Out in 1993 – back in for 1995.

Goalie	Miller	£3.0 million
Defender	Vickers	£3.2 million
Defender	Whyte	£2.7 million
Forward	Fjortoft	£3.3 million
Forward	Pollock	£2.8 million
Forward	Hendrie	£3.0 million

⊛Newcastle United
Kevin Keegan's cracking collection.

Goalie	Srnicek	£2.7 million
Defender	Beresford	£2.8 million
Defender	Hottiger	£2.8 million
Forward	Beardsley	£3.5 million
Forward	Fox	£3.1 million
Forward	Gillespie	£3.3 million

⊛Nottingham Forest
The Reds – a colourful collection.

Goalie	Crossley	£3.0 million
Defender	Cooper	£3.0 million

Defender	Pearce	£3.3 million
Forward	Collymore	£3.7 million
Forward	Roy	£3.4 million
Forward	Woan	£2.9 million

⊛ Queens Park Rangers
A right royal selection.

Goalie	Roberts	£2.4 million
Defender	Bardsley	£2.6 million
Defender	Maddix	£2.2 million
Forward	Ferdinand	£2.8 million
Forward	Impey	£2.4 million
Forward	Holloway	£2.3 million

⊛ Sheffield Wednesday
The Owls – winging their way to the top.

Goalie	Woods	£1.8 million
Defender	Atherton	£2.1 million
Defender	Walker	£1.6 million
Forward	Bright	£2.4 million
Forward	Waddle	£1.9 million
Forward	Sinton	£1.7 million

⊛ Southampton
Choose a Dell-boy or two!

Goalie	Grobbelaar	£2.4 million
Defender	Dodd	£2.3 million
Defender	Hall	£2.2 million
Forward	Le Tissier	£3.3 million
Forward	Maddison	£1.9 million
Forward	Magilton	£2.4 million

✪ Tottenham Hotspur
Hot stuff from the Spurs.

Goalie	Walker	£2.6 million
Defender	Austin	£2.9 million
Defender	Calderwood	£2.7 million
Forward	Rosenthal	£2.4 million
Forward	Sheringham	£3.1 million
Forward	Barmby	£2.9 million

✪ West Ham United
Nearly went south – can they improve?

Goalie	Miklosko	£1.4 million
Defender	Breacker	£1.7 million
Defender	Potts	£1.2 million
Forward	Cottee	£2.0 million
Forward	Moncur	£1.5 million
Forward	Boere	£1.1 million

✪ Wimbledon
Serve up a racquet with the Dons.

Goalie	Segers	£1.9 million
Defender	Elkins	£2.4 million
Defender	Kimble	£2.2 million
Forward	Ekoku	£2.7 million
Forward	Holdsworth	£2.5 million
Forward	Jones	£2.1 million

If one of the named players moves to another club, his value stays the same. Don't take his price from the Bargain Basement.

✪ BARGAIN BASEMENT BONANZA! ✪

If you've been searching for your favourite footie star and can't find him – don't panic! Any Premiership player can be picked for your team. If he doesn't appear in either of the two previous sections, then his value just depends on the club he plays for. Check out the list and pick up some bargains.

Team played for	Cost per player
Arsenal	£1.8 million
Aston Villa	£0.6 million
Blackburn Rovers	£3.2 million
Bolton Wanderers	£1.4 million
Chelsea	£1.9 million
Coventry City	£0.7 million
Everton	£1.2 million
Leeds United	£2.5 million
Liverpool	£2.7 million
Manchester City	£0.6 million
Manchester United	£3.0 million
Middlesborough	£2.5 million
Newcastle United	£2.4 million
Nottingham Forest	£2.6 million
Queens Park Rangers	£1.9 million

Sheffield Wednesday	£1.4 million
Southampton	£1.6 million
Tottenham Hotspur	£2.2 million
West Ham United	£1.0 million
Wimbledon	£1.5 million

COST OF TEAM

PLAYERS	TEAM	COST
Seaman	Arsenal	2,800,000
Flixcroft	man. city	0.8500,000
Ehioge	Aston villa	0.7
	Total Cost	
	Money left over	

TRANSFER PIGGY BANK.

SORRY! Any money you have left over doesn't go in your back pocket. No Premiership manager would behave like that — well, none of the ones who are left, anyway. You can use your spare cash for transfers later in the season.

JEFF'S TOP TIPS

⊗ Not sure who to sign?

⊗ Planning on pulling the names out of a hat?

⊗ Don't make another move until you've listened to Jeff!

Now, I know referees shouldn't take sides but it's time you had a helping hand.

For the next 38 weeks of the Premiership you'll be battling it out with 20 top teams and you need a squad you can rely on. So here are a few suggestions to help you lead the League!

1. Go for goals
If you want to be the best — if you want to beat the rest — you don't just need dedication. You also need a team that can hammer the ball into the back of the net. So, when you're picking your forwards you should select as many strikers as possible. Midfielders will score you points if they pass the ball up to a goal-scorer, but not as many as the goal-scorer will himself.

2. Points for penalties

Most Premiership sides have
one or two players who
regularly take penalty kicks.
You'll be guaranteed to get
some goals if you sign up
some of these. Sometimes,
the perfect penalty placers
are defenders — a must
for your back four!

3. Research brings rewards

You'll probably spend time doing your sums to see how
many of the big names you can afford. But what about
some of the names we haven't listed? Deep in the depths
of the **Bargain Basement** are some fantastic footballers.
To prove it, pick one of the top three Clubs from last
season and try to name as many of their players as
possible. Chances are you'll have just found some
brilliant bargains.

It's also worth following all the transfer dealings in the
summer. Foreign players signed at the last minute can all
be found in the **Bargain Basement.** Last season,
Fantasy Team players could have snapped up Jürgen
Klinsmann for a measly £1.3 million! What a gift!

4. Stars not subs

Your players only score points for you when they're on the field, so they must have a regular place in the team. If you choose someone who spends his time on the subs' bench, you'll be throwing your money away. You'll also disappear from the League table faster than you can say Ilie Dumitrescu!

Also avoid players who are regularly red-carded or who suffer from a lot of injuries. And it's always best to go for players who tackle the opposition not the spectators.

When you're happy with your squad, write their names in the first Score Chart on page 58. Also write down the Premiership side they play for. This will help you when you're filling in your scores. Now you're ready to lead your team to goals and glory — or red cards and relegation.

Good luck!

Chapter Three

✪ HOW YOU SCORE ✪

LET'S GET THE GAME UNDERWAY!

Understanding the scoring system is an absolute doddle. Getting a good score, on the other hand, isn't so easy. It all depends on how the players you've picked perform in real Premiership games.

If you've got a side full of hot shots, you'll earn points galore. But if your team boasts more left feet than a caterpillar, things could be very different!

Fantasy Team veterans will already know the scoring basics. Even so, it's essential **all** managers read this chapter. The new season means several **NEW RULES** and if you don't brush up on the regulations you could fall foul of Jeff the Ref!

Check out the NEW RULES for the 1995-96 season.

A FEW POINTS ABOUT POINTS

First the good news. Every time one of your players scores for his club in a Premiership game he scores for your side too. Result! But before you start a lap of honour round the living room, wait till you hear the bad news.

As well as earning points for a good performance, your players can lose them if they don't play well. Each goal scored against the Premiership team of one of your players costs your *Fantasy Team* valuable points – and that can spell disaster!

The success or failure of your *Fantasy Team* depends on the actual performance of your players in real games. But remember it's only the scores in Premiership matches which count. Although you can pick up extra bonus points if your players appear in internationals or cup finals, the scores of these games are not included in your weekly Fantasy Team Total.

HE SHOOTS – HE SCORES!

Players can win (and lose!) points for your *Fantasy Team* in several ways:

Scoring goals (all players)

Every time one of your players wallops the ball into the back of the net he scores **four points (+4)** for your team. Unless of course it's his own net he wallops the ball into! An own goal means **minus four points (–4)**.

No goals (forwards only)

Your strikers and midfield players are there to get goals not a sun tan! If no member of your team scores during the week, all the forwards have **minus one point (–1)** deducted from their total.

Conceding goals (defenders and goalie only)

Your defenders and goalie are meant to stop other sides scoring. Each goal scored against their team counts as **minus two points (–2)** against your *Fantasy Team*.

Clean sheet (defenders and goalie only)

Your defence can earn points for your side too. Every time one of them plays a match without conceding a single goal they add a useful **four points (+4)** to your weekly total.

⊛ Missing more than 4 matches (all players)

Players who miss games are worse than useless. After skipping four games in a row, a missing player then costs your team **minus four points (–4) every match** until he's back on the pitch!

All of the above are **individual** player points. But as well as playing brilliantly as individuals, each of your players contributes to the overall performance of his team. They may help set up goals but not score them, and if their side does badly they must share the blame. So the result of each of their **team's** games is included in your Fantasy Team Total.

⊛ Premiership result (all players)

Every goal scored by your players' real-life teams is worth **one point (+1)** to your side. In the same way, every goal let in by their teams costs your side **minus one point (–1)**.

CHARTING YOUR SUCCESS

To help you work out how many points your *Fantasy Team* has scored, there are nifty Score Charts. You'll find them on pages 55-107 and there's one for each week of the football season. To show you how to use them, on page 37 we have filled in a Score Chart showing one week's imaginary results for our *Fantasy Team* – REVENGE ROVERS.

It's a result!

All you have to do is make a note of the points your players earn between the dates given at the top of each Score Chart. Then at the end of the week just add all their points together and – bingo! – you've got your weekly **Fantasy Team Total** score. Nothing could be easier – and to prove it, we'll show you how it works!

Take my advice and get yourself a fixtures list showing the dates of all the Premiership matches and which teams are playing. That way you won't miss any results.

Lots of newspapers print a list at the beginning of the season. You can also buy one from the F.A. For details, phone or write to:

The Football Association,
16 Lancaster Gate,
London W2 3LW.
Telephone: 0171 262 4542

Before we can start scoring, we need some results – so we've made some up! You'll be able to get the real footie results from newspapers, radio and TV.

Monday 13 November

Manchester City 1 *(Rosler)*, Leeds United 0

Middlesborough 0, Manchester United 0

Wednesday 15 November

Newcastle United 2 *(Beardsley, Fox)*, Arsenal 0

Saturday 18 November

Liverpool 0, Everton 2 *(Limpar 2)*

Queens Park Rangers 0, Southampton 3 *(Magilton 2, Hall)*

Aston Villa 1 *(Yorke)*, Coventry City 1 *(Wegerle)*

Wimbledon 1 *(Ekoku)*, Chelsea 0

Tottenham Hotspur 0, Nottingham Forest 2 *(Roy, Woan)*

Blackburn Rovers 2 *(Sutton, Shearer)*, Leeds United 1 *(Yeboah)*

OK, so let's see what these results would mean for our team, Revenge Rovers. First let's look at our defenders and goalie.

Our goalie, Coton, plays for Manchester City – and we're off to a good start! His clean sheet gives him four points **(+4)**. And don't forget to add a point **(+1)** in his team column for Manchester City's goal. So Coton notches up a terrific five points.

Winterburn has let us down this week as Arsenal were beaten 2–0. In his individual column he gets minus two points for each goal conceded, which comes to –4. In his team column he gets minus one point for each goal conceded, so that comes to –2. His tragic total is minus six!

The goal scored against Aston Villa in their one-all draw means minus two (**–2**) for Staunton in his individual points column. In his team points column he gets a minus point (**–1**) for the goal conceded and a plus point (**+1**) for the goal scored.

Sinclair let a goal in too! Chelsea's 1–0 defeat at the hands (or rather feet) of Wimbledon means minus two (**–2**) in his individual points and minus one (**–1**) in his team points.

So far, our Revenge Rovers are on a pathetic minus six. It's a good job these are only imaginary results! Let's see if our forwards can save the day.

Pollock didn't score against Manchester United – but at least the 0–0 result means he didn't earn us any more minus points! His score this week is zero.

At last – some plus points! Limpar walloped home

both goals in his match and gets a glorious four points for each one **(+8)** in his individual points column. The final score of 2–0 also means he gets two points **(+2)** in his team total and no minus points!

Le Tissier didn't score any of the goals in Southampton's 3–0 victory over Queens Park Rangers, so he gets no individual points. Even so, he still gets plus three points **(+3)** in his team points column for the three goals scored by his team mates.

Sheringham, on the other hand, failed to score – and so did the rest of the team! And as they lost 2–0, he ends up with minus two **(–2)** team points.

Finally, Shearer for Blackburn Rovers got one of the goals in their 2–1 win over Leeds United. Which means he gets four individual points **(+4)**, while in his team points column he gets plus two points **(+2)** and minus one **(–1)**, making his overall score five.

That's all the results, so let's have a look at our Score Chart. Once you've worked out each player's total score, just add them all together to get your Fantasy Team Total. As you can see from the completed Score Chart, Revenge Rovers ended up with ten points this week.

SCORE CHART: 13 NOV - 19 NOV

POSITION	PLAYER TEAM	INDIVIDUAL		TEAM		TOTAL
		Plus	Minus	Plus	Minus	
Goalie	Coton/Manchester City	+4	O	+1	O	+5
Defence	Winterburn/Arsenal	O	-4	O	-2	-6
Defence	Staunton/Aston Villa	O	-2	+1	-1	-2
Defence	Walker/Sheffield Wednesday	O	O	O	O	O
Defence	Sinclair/Chelsea	O	-2	O	-1	-3
Forward	Pollock/Middlesborough	O	O	O	O	O
Forward	Limpar/Everton	+8	O	+2	O	+10
Forward	*LeTissier/Southampton	O	O	+3	O	+3
Forward	Cottee/West Ham	O	O	O	O	O
Forward	Sheringham/Tottenham Hotspur	O	O	O	-2	-2
Forward	*Shearer/Blackburn Rovers	+4	O	+2	-1	+5

REVENGE ROVERS FANTASY TEAM TOTAL

☆ BONUS BONANZA: Mega Manager	Footie Forecast ✕	On the Ball ✕
		WEEKLY FANTASY TOTAL

Result of Match ....

League Points awarded ....

League total so far ....

Top of the League this week .... points

Bottom of the League this week .... points

This week my team is .... in the League

WHERE WERE YOU?

You'll notice two of our players didn't get a game this week because their teams weren't in any matches. No problem! All the top teams end up playing exactly the same number of League games. Those that missed out this week will play an extra match later on and catch up.

On the other hand a player who isn't selected for his team *is* a problem! After missing four games in a row he will cost you **minus four points** every time his team plays without him. If this happens you should think about a transfer — so check out Chapter Five!

JEFF THE REF'S BONUS BONANZA

There's just one more bit about scoring left to explain. Jeff the Ref's bonus points were so popular last season, he's come up with some more. Now there are three categories: **Footie Forecasts**, **Mega Manager**, and **On the Ball**. They give you the chance to earn up to two extra points for your side each week. But you'll have to work hard for them!

⊗ FOOTIE FORECASTS

How do you rate the chances of England, Scotland and Wales this year? Peer into your crystal (foot)ball and see if you can predict the results of the games listed at the beginning of the Score Charts (*page 57*). Write what you think the match results will be on your Footie Forecast chart. Each one you guess right will earn you two bonus points **(+2)**. If you get the scores wrong but predict the winning team, award yourself one bonus point **(+1)**.

⊗ MEGA MANAGER

Good managers keep a close eye on their players – not just the match results! And that dedication really pays off with the chance to scoop all sorts of bonuses. So give yourself a pat on the back and one point extra, for any one of the following:

- ⊗ you go along to a match and see one of your players in action.

- ⊗ one of your players takes part in an international match or cup final.

- ⊗ your goalie saves a penalty in a League game.

- ⊗ one of your players is named man of the match.

- ⊗ one of your players scores the winning goal in extra time.

⊗ ON THE BALL

As manager, you're the brains of the team and soon those brains will be put to the test. Hidden among the Score Charts are some fiendishly tricky puzzles and each one is worth a brilliant bonus. But only if you get it right! Don't bother looking for them now – wait until you come to the right week. Besides you've got more than enough to think about already!

REMEMBER!

Jeff's generosity isn't limitless! You may award yourself no more than two bonus points each week. Any extra bonuses don't count and you can't carry bonus points over into the next week's results.

A FINAL REMINDER

That just about wraps it up as far as scoring is concerned. Told you it was a doddle! In the next chapter you'll find out how to turn your team's score into a match result. In other words whether you won, lost or drew that week's game.

But before we get into all of that let's just go over the scoring basics one more time.

SCORING SUMMARY

Player scores a goal.	**+4 points** per goal.
Player scores an own goal.	**−4 points** per goal.
No goals scored all week.	**−1 point** deducted from every forward.
Clean sheet (defender or goalie concedes no goals).	**+4 points** every match.
Defender or goalie concedes goal.	**−2 points** per goal.
Player misses four games in a row.	**−4 points** for each subsequent missed match until he is back on the pitch.
Player's team scores.	**+1 point.**
Player's team concedes a goal.	**−1 point.**

And don't forget the BONUS BONANZA. You can win up to TWO extra points.

Chapter Four

RACE FOR THE PREMIERSHIP

IT'S TIME TO TAKE ON THE PROFESSIONALS!

OK, so you've learned how to score. But what do all your players' points add up to? A place in the Premiership – that's what! Yes, it's time to join the table of our greatest teams and find out just how good your side really is.

Your *Fantasy Team* plays one match every week. And at the end of each week you can see the result of the game just by looking at your **Weekly Fantasy Total**. To work out the result simply add all your players' scores together plus any bonus points you might have earned. Now what have you got?

- **Eleven points or more** and you'll be dancing in the dug-out while your fans tango on the terraces. You've won! This glorious victory earns your team three Premiership points. Congratulations!

- **Between minus ten and nine points** means a draw and one League point. Things could be worse – but they could be better too. Who knows – a couple of Jeff the Ref bonus points might have made all the difference!

- **Less than minus ten** – hang your head in shame. You've lost and (you guessed it) that means your team don't earn any points on the League table. Still there's always next week!

ON TEN–DER HOOKS

Hang on a minute, you're thinking, what if my team scores 10 points? Well, last season in *Fantasy Team*, 10 points would have automatically meant the game was a draw. But this year we're giving you a final shot at winning the match – in a penalty shoot out!

Back in Chapter Two when you picked your team we asked you to choose two players as your Penalty Powerhouse. Now you know why. If your team ends up with exactly ten points at the end of any week, these two sharp shooters along  with your goalie are going to have to save the day.

You can still snatch victory – but only if your Penalty Powerhouse players have managed to score more goals than your goalie let in. So even if they scored two each but your goalie conceded four or more the match would remain a draw.

YOUR PREMIER POSITION

As soon as you've worked out the match result, add the number of League points your side has earned to your League Total on the Score Chart. As the season continues your overall total will grow – providing of course you don't lose all your matches!

Each week, make a note on the Score Chart of your team's position in the League table, who's leading the League and which side is bottom. At a glance you'll be able to see how your *Fantasy Team* compares to champion sides like Manchester United and Blackburn Rovers. Will you be soaring to the top of the League table, or racing towards the relegation zone? Only time will tell!

CHECK IT OUT

Look at our completed Score Chart. Revenge Rovers'
score of ten means it's time for a penalty shoot out!
Let's say we had selected Le Tissier and Shearer as our
Penalty Powerhouse. Le Tissier didn't score this week,
Shearer hammered home one goal, and our goalie
didn't let in any goals. So, our Penalty Powerhouse
scored one more goal than our goalie conceded. That's
a win for Revenge Rovers and three League points.
We're pretending (with our imaginary results!) that
we've got 17 points so far this season. With this week's
result we have a terrific twenty League points.

SCORE CHART: 13 NOV - 19 NOV

POSITION	PLAYER TEAM	INDIVIDUAL		TEAM		TOTAL
		Plus	Minus	Plus	Minus	
Goalie	Coton/Manchester City	+4	O	+1	O	+5
Defence	Winterburn/Arsenal	O	−4	O	−2	−6
Defence	Staunton/Aston Villa	O	−2	+1	−1	−2
Defence	Walker/Sheffield Wednesday	O	O	O	O	O
Defence	Sinclair/Chelsea	O	−2	O	−1	−3
Forward	Pollock/Middlesborough	O	O	O	O	O
Forward	Limpar/Everton	+8	O	+2	O	+10
Forward	* Le Tissier/Southampton	O	O	+3	O	+3
Forward	Cottee/West Ham	O	O	O	O	O
Forward	Sheringham/Tottenham Hotspur	O	O	O	−2	−2
Forward	* Shearer/Blackburn Rovers	+4	O	+2	−1	+5

REVENGE ROVERS	FANTASY TEAM TOTAL	10

☆BONUS BONANZA: Mega Manager	O	Footie Forecast	✗	On the Ball	✗	O

	WEEKLY FANTASY TOTAL	10

Result of Match ..... Win ....

League Points awarded ..... 3 ....

League total so far ..... 20 ....

Top of the League this week ... Middlesborough .... 30 ... points

Bottom of the League this week ... Aston Villa .... 11 ... points

This week my team is ... 10th ... in the League

LATE KICK–OFF

What if you want to start playing *Fantasy Team* after the beginning of the football season? All the other teams in the Premiership will have started scoring. But don't panic – we're on the case!

To help you catch up, there are the **Late Kick-off Quiz** questions starting on page 110. You have to tackle two of these fiendish football teasers for each week you miss. If you get both answers right then you've won that week's game – award yourself three League points on the Score Chart. If you get one right, the game was a draw and you gain one point. And if you get both answers wrong, you lose and get no points on that week's chart. Work your way through the questions, filling in the Score Charts until you come to the first complete week that your team can start playing.

During the weeks you play the **Late Kick-off Quiz,** you can ignore the **On the Ball** quizzes you will find amongst the Score Chart. They won't change your score. However, if you want, you could use them to brush up on your footie know-how. But when you start playing *Fantasy Team* properly, you can gain some extra bonus points by doing these tricky teasers

Chapter Five

MAKING TRANSFERS

When the season starts you'll quickly see what sort of team you've picked. You'll know you've chosen well when those plus points start piling up every week. But what about the players who let you down? Perhaps you've picked a schmuck instead of a Schmeichel as your goalie. Or your magnificent midfielder is more Graham Slow than Gary Speed. Well, you do what any caring, understanding manager would do – kick them out!

SWAP SHOP

Yup – we're giving you TWO chances to change your team and bring in new talent. On each occasion you can replace as many as three of your players. That means over half your side can be replaced – which could turn them from wimps into winners!

Your two transfer opportunities can be made at the start of any *Fantasy Team* week. But don't use them both at the start of the season — you've got a tough 38 weeks ahead of you.

ALL CHANGE

Now get ready for a shock! The values of all your squad members change during the season. The better a player is the more you can sell him for. A great goal scorer will see his transfer value zoom upwards. But a gormless goalie will be worth less than you paid for him. That means to get rid of a useless player you may also have to sell a brilliant one!

HOW IT ALL ADDS UP

To find out a player's current value, add up all the points he has won or lost so far. Each point is worth £10,000 on the transfer market, so multiply the total by 10,000. Add this figure to the player's original price to get his transfer value.

Here's how it works:
You bought Danny Defender for £2 million. After ten weeks he is your top-scoring player with 30 points.

So he is now worth an extra £300,000 (30 x 10,000). His transfer value is £2,300,000 (£2,000,000 + £300,000).

Sammy Striker is a dismal failure. He only cost you £800,000 but he's scored −80 points so far. The change in his value is −£800,000 (−80 x 10,000). This means he's worth nothing (800,000 − 800,000 = 0)!

A player can never be worth less than nothing. If Sammy had scored −100 points his value would still be £0.00.

SELLING PLAYERS

1. Choose which players you want to sell. Remember there's a maximum of three each time.
2. Work out their new transfer values. Add up the total money you will receive for them.
3. Sack them!

BUYING PLAYERS

You will now have one, two or three spaces in your team. These can be filled with any Premiership player – as long as you can afford them. The good news is that their prices haven't changed – all players still cost the same as in Chapter Two.

1. Work out how much money you have. If you had any money left over when you bought your original squad, now is the time to use it. Just add it to the money you received from selling your players.

2. Choose which players you want from Chapter Two. Make sure they don't come to more than the money in your kitty.

3. Change the names of players in the Score Chart from the week you buy them.

REMEMBER! After you have bought and sold you must still have one goalie, four defenders and six forwards. And no more than three players from any one Premiership side!

POINTLESS PEOPLE

It's not just poor performers you should think about transferring. Any of your team who end up as substitutes for their club or have serious injuries should be dropped. Don't forget, if they miss more than four games they'll lose points each time they miss another match.

Each of your new signings will earn points for you from the week they are picked. Whatever they've done before doesn't count, so make sure they're not running out of steam before you buy them.

SCORE CHARTS

1995/96

My team name:

_____

SCORING SUMMARY
A QUICK REMINDER OF THE BASICS

Player scores a goal.	**+4 points** per goal.
Player scores an own goal.	**–4 points** per goal.
No goals scored all week. forward.	**–1 point** from every
Clean sheet (defender or goalie concedes no goals).	**+4 points** every match.
Player misses four games in a row.	**–4 points** for each subsequent missed match until he is back on the pitch.
Defender or goalie concedes goal.	**–2 points** per goal.
Player's team scores.	**+1 point.**
Player's team concedes a goal.	**–1 point.**

FOOTIE FORECASTS

Here's your chance to win some valuable points. Fill in the result you predict for the three matches below. If you forecast correctly, you can award yourself two bonus points (+2) on your Score Chart for that week. If you get the score wrong but have forecast the winning team, add one bonus point (+1).

DATE	MATCH	YOUR FORECAST	RESULT
6 Sept	Wales v. Moldavia		
11 Oct	Norway v. England		
15 Nov	Scotland v. San Marino		

If the footie season has already begun, check out the **Late Kick-off Quiz** questions from page 110. Come on, there's no time to lose!

*Mark your 2 Penalty Powerhouse players.

SCORE CHART: 14 Aug - 20 Aug

POSITION	PLAYER	TEAM	INDIVIDUAL		TEAM		TOTAL
			Plus	Minus	Plus	Minus	
Goalie							
Defence							
Defence							
Defence							
Defence							
Forward							
Forward							
Forward							
Forward							
Forward							
Forward							
					FANTASY TEAM TOTAL		
☆ BONUS BONANZA: Mega Manager			Footie Forecast	✕	On the Ball	✕	
					WEEKLY FANTASY TOTAL		

Result of Match . . . .

League Points awarded . . . .

League total so far . . . .

Top of the League this week . . . . points

Bottom of the League this week . . . . points

This week my team is . . . . in the League

SCORE CHART: 21 Aug - 27 Aug

POSITION	PLAYER TEAM	INDIVIDUAL		TEAM		TOTAL
		Plus	Minus	Plus	Minus	
Goalie						
Defence						
Defence						
Defence						
Defence						
Forward						
Forward						
Forward						
Forward						
Forward						
Forward						

FANTASY TEAM TOTAL

☆ BONUS BONANZA: Mega Manager | Footie Forecast ☒ | On the Ball ☒

WEEKLY FANTASY TOTAL

Result of Match ....

League Points awarded ....

League total so far ....

Top of the League this week .... points

Bottom of the League this week .... points

This week my team is .... in the League

ON THE BALL

Chaos! The ball is lost!?
You have 30 seconds to track it
down so play can re-start. If you
find it in time award your team a
bonus point for the week
28 Aug — 3 Sept.

SCORE CHART: 28 Aug - 3 Sept

POSITION	PLAYER	TEAM	INDIVIDUAL		TEAM		TOTAL
			Plus	Minus	Plus	Minus	
Goalie							
Defence							
Defence							
Defence							
Defence							
Forward							
Forward							
Forward							
Forward							
Forward							
Forward							
				FANTASY TEAM TOTAL			
☆ BONUS BONANZA: Mega Manager		Footie Forecast	╳	On the Ball			
				WEEKLY FANTASY TOTAL			

Result of Match . . . .

League Points awarded . . . .

League total so far . . . .

Top of the League this week . . . . points

Bottom of the League this week . . . . points

This week my team is . . . . in the League

SCORE CHART: 4 Sept - 10 Sept

POSITION	PLAYER	TEAM	INDIVIDUAL		TEAM		TOTAL
			Plus	Minus	Plus	Minus	
Goalie							
Defence							
Defence							
Defence							
Defence							
Forward							
Forward							
Forward							
Forward							
Forward							
Forward							

FANTASY TEAM TOTAL

☆ BONUS BONANZA: Mega Manager | Footie Forecast | On the Ball ✕

WEEKLY FANTASY TOTAL

Result of Match . . . .

League Points awarded . . . .

League total so far . . . .

Top of the League this week . . . . points

Bottom of the League this week . . . . points

This week my team is . . . . in the League

☆ **Remember to check your Footie Forecast this week.**

SCORE CHART: 11 Sept - 17 Sept

POSITION	PLAYER	TEAM	INDIVIDUAL		TEAM		TOTAL
			Plus	Minus	Plus	Minus	
Goalie							
Defence							
Defence							
Defence							
Defence							
Forward							
Forward							
Forward							
Forward							
Forward							
Forward							

FANTASY TEAM TOTAL		
☆ BONUS BONANZA: Mega Manager	Footie Forecast ☒ On the Ball ☒	
WEEKLY FANTASY TOTAL		

Result of Match . . . .

League Points awarded . . . .

League total so far . . . .

Top of the League this week . . . . points

Bottom of the League this week . . . . points

This week my team is . . . . in the League

SCORE CHART: 18 Sept - 24 Sept

POSITION	PLAYER	TEAM	INDIVIDUAL		TEAM		TOTAL
			Plus	Minus	Plus	Minus	
Goalie							
Defence							
Defence							
Defence							
Defence							
Forward							
Forward							
Forward							
Forward							
Forward							
Forward							

FANTASY TEAM TOTAL

☆ BONUS BONANZA: Mega Manager | Footie Forecast ☒ | On the Ball ☒

WEEKLY FANTASY TOTAL

Result of Match ....

League Points awarded ....

League total so far ....

Top of the League this week .... points

Bottom of the League this week .... points

This week my team is .... in the League

SCORE CHART: 25 Sept - 1 Oct

POSITION	PLAYER	TEAM	INDIVIDUAL		TEAM		TOTAL
			Plus	Minus	Plus	Minus	
Goalie							
Defence							
Defence							
Defence							
Defence							
Forward							
Forward							
Forward							
Forward							
Forward							
Forward							
				FANTASY TEAM TOTAL			
☆ BONUS BONANZA: Mega Manager			Footie Forecast	✕	On the Ball	✕	
				WEEKLY FANTASY TOTAL			

Result of Match . . . .

League Points awarded . . . .

League total so far . . . .

Top of the League this week . . . . points

Bottom of the League this week . . . . points

This week my team is . . . . in the League

ON THE BALL

GOAAAAL! Or is it? Where's the ball? Spot it within 30 seconds and you've earned your team an extra bonus point for the week 2 Oct - 8 Oct.

SCORE CHART: 2 Oct - 8 Oct

POSITION	PLAYER	TEAM	INDIVIDUAL Plus	INDIVIDUAL Minus	TEAM Plus	TEAM Minus	TOTAL
Goalie							
Defence							
Defence							
Defence							
Defence							
Forward							
Forward							
Forward							
Forward							
Forward							
Forward							

FANTASY TEAM TOTAL

☆ BONUS BONANZA: Mega Manager ☐ Footie Forecast ☒ On the Ball

WEEKLY FANTASY TOTAL

Result of Match ....

League Points awarded ....

League total so far ....

Top of the League this week .... points

Bottom of the League this week .... points

This week my team is .... in the League

SCORE CHART: 9 Oct - 15 Oct

POSITION	PLAYER	TEAM	INDIVIDUAL		TEAM		TOTAL
			Plus	Minus	Plus	Minus	
Goalie							
Defence							
Defence							
Defence							
Defence							
Forward							
Forward							
Forward							
Forward							
Forward							
Forward							
			FANTASY TEAM TOTAL				
☆ BONUS BONANZA: Mega Manager			Footie Forecast		On the Ball		
			WEEKLY FANTASY TOTAL				

Result of Match ....

League Points awarded ....

League total so far ....

Top of the League this week ....points

Bottom of the League this week ....points

This week my team is .... in the League

☆ **Remember to check your Footie Forecast this week.**

SCORE CHART: 16 Oct - 22 Oct

POSITION	PLAYER	TEAM	INDIVIDUAL		TEAM		TOTAL
			Plus	Minus	Plus	Minus	
Goalie							
Defence							
Defence							
Defence							
Defence							
Forward							
Forward							
Forward							
Forward							
Forward							
Forward							

FANTASY TEAM TOTAL

☆ BONUS BONANZA: Mega Manager | Footie Forecast ✕ | On the Ball ✕

WEEKLY FANTASY TOTAL

Result of Match . . . .

League Points awarded . . . .

League total so far . . . .

Top of the League this week . . . . points

Bottom of the League this week . . . . points

This week my team is . . . . in the League

ON THE BALL

Time to test your brain power. Just how much do you know about the rules of the game? Find out by tackling Jeff's teaser. For each answer you get right, award yourself one extra bonus point for the week 23 Oct – 29 Oct.

1. JEFF THE STRIKER!
It's the dying seconds of the Cup Final.

Sunbridge are on the attack.

And it's a terrific header – from the referee.

Come on Ref, have we scored?

Question: Jeff didn't see the goal, neither did his linesman. What should he do?

    A. *Award the goal.*

    B. *Give Sunbridge a free kick.*

    C. *Re-start the game with a dropped ball.*

2. From which of these can a goal be scored direct?

    A. *A goal kick.*

    B. *A corner kick.*

    C. *A place kick.*

ANSWERS

1. C. Jeff cannot award the goal because he did not see it clearly. He should first ask a neutral linesman if the goal should stand. If neither of the linesmen saw it, then a dropped ball is used to re-start the game.

2. B. A corner kick.

I have scored _____ Bonus Bonanza points.

			INDIVIDUAL		TEAM		
SCORE CHART: 23 Oct - 29 Oct							
POSITION	PLAYER	TEAM	Plus	Minus	Plus	Minus	TOTAL
Goalie							
Defence							
Defence							
Defence							
Defence							
Forward							
Forward							
Forward							
Forward							
Forward							
Forward							
			FANTASY TEAM TOTAL				
☆ BONUS BONANZA: Mega Manager			Footie Forecast ✕		On the Ball		
			WEEKLY FANTASY TOTAL				

Result of Match ....

League Points awarded ....

League total so far ....

Top of the League this week .... points

Bottom of the League this week .... points

This week my team is .... in the League

SCORE CHART: 30 Oct - 5 Nov

POSITION	PLAYER	TEAM	INDIVIDUAL		TEAM		TOTAL
			Plus	Minus	Plus	Minus	
Goalie							
Defence							
Defence							
Defence							
Defence							
Forward							
Forward							
Forward							
Forward							
Forward							
Forward							

		FANTASY TEAM TOTAL			
☆ BONUS BONANZA: Mega Manager		Footie Forecast ✕	On the Ball ✕		
		WEEKLY FANTASY TOTAL			

Result of Match ....

League Points awarded ....

League total so far ....

Top of the League this week .... points

Bottom of the League this week .... points

This week my team is .... in the League

SCORE CHART: 6 Nov - 12 Nov

POSITION	PLAYER	TEAM	INDIVIDUAL		TEAM		TOTAL
			Plus	Minus	Plus	Minus	
Goalie							
Defence							
Defence							
Defence							
Defence							
Forward							
Forward							
Forward							
Forward							
Forward							
Forward							

FANTASY TEAM TOTAL

☆ BONUS BONANZA: Mega Manager | Footie Forecast ☒ | On the Ball ☒

WEEKLY FANTASY TOTAL

Result of Match ....

League Points awarded ....

League total so far ....

Top of the League this week .... points

Bottom of the League this week .... points

This week my team is .... in the League

SCORE CHART: 13 Nov - 19 Nov

POSITION	PLAYER	TEAM	INDIVIDUAL Plus	INDIVIDUAL Minus	TEAM Plus	TEAM Minus	TOTAL
Goalie							
Defence							
Defence							
Defence							
Defence							
Forward							
Forward							
Forward							
Forward							
Forward							
Forward							

FANTASY TEAM TOTAL

☆ BONUS BONANZA: Mega Manager | Footie Forecast | On the Ball ✕

WEEKLY FANTASY TOTAL

Result of Match ....

League Points awarded ....

League total so far ....

Top of the League this week .... points

Bottom of the League this week .... points

This week my team is .... in the League

 Remember to check your Footie Forecast this week.

75

SCORE CHART: 20 Nov - 26 Nov

POSITION	PLAYER	TEAM	INDIVIDUAL		TEAM		TOTAL
			Plus	Minus	Plus	Minus	
Goalie							
Defence							
Defence							
Defence							
Defence							
Forward							
Forward							
Forward							
Forward							
Forward							
Forward							

FANTASY TEAM TOTAL

☆ BONUS BONANZA: Mega Manager | Footie Forecast ☒ | On the Ball ☒

WEEKLY FANTASY TOTAL

Result of Match . . . .

League Points awarded . . . .

League total so far . . . .

Top of the League this week . . . . points

Bottom of the League this week . . . . points

This week my team is . . . . in the League

SCORE CHART: 27 Nov - 3 Dec

POSITION	PLAYER	TEAM	INDIVIDUAL		TEAM		TOTAL
			Plus	Minus	Plus	Minus	
Goalie							
Defence							
Defence							
Defence							
Defence							
Forward							
Forward							
Forward							
Forward							
Forward							
Forward							
				FANTASY TEAM TOTAL			
☆ BONUS BONANZA: Mega Manager			Footie Forecast ✕		On the Ball ✕		
				WEEKLY FANTASY TOTAL			

Result of Match ....

League Points awarded ....

League total so far ....

Top of the League this week .... points

Bottom of the League this week .... points

This week my team is .... in the League

SCORE CHART: 4 Dec - 10 Dec

POSITION	PLAYER	TEAM	INDIVIDUAL		TEAM		TOTAL
			Plus	Minus	Plus	Minus	
Goalie							
Defence							
Defence							
Defence							
Defence							
Forward							
Forward							
Forward							
Forward							
Forward							
Forward							

FANTASY TEAM TOTAL

☆ BONUS BONANZA: Mega Manager   Footie Forecast ✗   On the Ball ✗

WEEKLY FANTASY TOTAL

Result of Match . . . .

League Points awarded . . . .

League total so far . . . .

Top of the League this week . . . . points

Bottom of the League this week . . . . points

This week my team is . . . . in the League

SCORE CHART: 11 Dec - 17 Dec

POSITION	PLAYER	TEAM	INDIVIDUAL		TEAM		TOTAL
			Plus	Minus	Plus	Minus	
Goalie							
Defence							
Defence							
Defence							
Defence							
Forward							
Forward							
Forward							
Forward							
Forward							
Forward							

FANTASY TEAM TOTAL

☆ BONUS BONANZA: Mega Manager | Footie Forecast ☒ | On the Ball ☒ |

WEEKLY FANTASY TOTAL

Result of Match ....

League Points awarded ....

League total so far ....

Top of the League this week .... points

Bottom of the League this week .... points

This week my team is .... in the League

SCORE CHART: 18 Dec - 24 Dec

POSITION	PLAYER	TEAM	INDIVIDUAL Plus	INDIVIDUAL Minus	TEAM Plus	TEAM Minus	TOTAL
Goalie							
Defence							
Defence							
Defence							
Defence							
Forward							
Forward							
Forward							
Forward							
Forward							
Forward							

FANTASY TEAM TOTAL

☆ BONUS BONANZA: Mega Manager ☐ Footie Forecast ☒ On the Ball ☒

WEEKLY FANTASY TOTAL

Result of Match . . . .

League Points awarded . . . .

League total so far . . . .

Top of the League this week . . . . points

Bottom of the League this week . . . . points

This week my team is . . . . in the League

80

SCORE CHART: 25 Dec - 31 Dec

POSITION	PLAYER	TEAM	INDIVIDUAL		TEAM		TOTAL
			Plus	Minus	Plus	Minus	
Goalie							
Defence							
Defence							
Defence							
Defence							
Forward							
Forward							
Forward							
Forward							
Forward							
Forward							
				FANTASY TEAM TOTAL			
☆ BONUS BONANZA: Mega Manager			Footie Forecast	✕	On the Ball	✕	
				WEEKLY FANTASY TOTAL			

Result of Match ....

League Points awarded ....

League total so far ....

Top of the League this week ....points

Bottom of the League this week ....points

This week my team is .... in the League

ON THE BALL

Thinking caps on! Here's another chance to give your team a boosting bonus. Pass this week's test with flying colours and you can add two extra points to your score for the week 1 Jan – 7 Jan.

1. FREE KICK FOUL-UP!

Hailstorm United have a free kick.

Sammy Striker decides to play it back.

Pity he didn't tell the goalie!

Question: It's an own goal from a free kick. What should Jeff do?

Don't tell me – I'm sure I know this one...

A. Let the goal stand.

B. Award a corner kick.

C. Get Sammy to take the free kick again.

2. A match is being decided by penalty kicks. Where should all the players be, apart from the player taking the kick and the two goalkeepers?

A. At least 10 yards from the penalty spot.

B. In the other half of the pitch.

C. In the centre circle.

I have scored _____ Bonus Bonanza points.

SCORE CHART: 1 Jan – 7 Jan

POSITION	PLAYER	TEAM	INDIVIDUAL		TEAM		TOTAL
			Plus	Minus	Plus	Minus	
Goalie							
Defence							
Defence							
Defence							
Defence							
Forward							
Forward							
Forward							
Forward							
Forward							
Forward							

FANTASY TEAM TOTAL	

☆ BONUS BONANZA: Mega Manager	Footie Forecast ✕ On the Ball	

WEEKLY FANTASY TOTAL	

Result of Match . . . .

League Points awarded . . . .

League total so far . . . .

Top of the League this week . . . . points

Bottom of the League this week . . . . points

This week my team is . . . . in the League

SCORE CHART: 8 Jan - 14 Jan

POSITION	PLAYER	TEAM	INDIVIDUAL		TEAM		TOTAL
			Plus	Minus	Plus	Minus	
Goalie							
Defence							
Defence							
Defence							
Defence							
Forward							
Forward							
Forward							
Forward							
Forward							
Forward							

FANTASY TEAM TOTAL

☆ BONUS BONANZA: Mega Manager | Footie Forecast ✕ | On the Ball ✕

WEEKLY FANTASY TOTAL

Result of Match . . . .

League Points awarded . . . .

League total so far . . . .

Top of the League this week . . . . points

Bottom of the League this week . . . . points

This week my team is . . . . in the League

ON THE BALL

SCORE CHART: 15 Jan - 21 Jan

POSITION	PLAYER	TEAM	INDIVIDUAL		TEAM		TOTAL
			Plus	Minus	Plus	Minus	
Goalie							
Defence							
Defence							
Defence							
Defence							
Forward							
Forward							
Forward							
Forward							
Forward							
Forward							
				FANTASY TEAM TOTAL			
☆ BONUS BONANZA: Mega Manager			Footie Forecast		On the Ball		
				WEEKLY FANTASY TOTAL			

Result of Match ....

League Points awarded ....

League total so far ....

Top of the League this week .... points

Bottom of the League this week .... points

This week my team is .... in the League

SCORE CHART: 22 Jan - 28 Jan

POSITION	PLAYER	TEAM	INDIVIDUAL		TEAM		TOTAL
			Plus	Minus	Plus	Minus	
Goalie							
Defence							
Defence							
Defence							
Defence							
Forward							
Forward							
Forward							
Forward							
Forward							
Forward							
				FANTASY TEAM TOTAL			
☆ BONUS BONANZA: Mega Manager			Footie Forecast ✗		On the Ball ✗		
				WEEKLY FANTASY TOTAL			

Result of Match ....

League Points awarded ....

League total so far ....

Top of the League this week .... points

Bottom of the League this week .... points

This week my team is .... in the League

SCORE CHART: 29 Jan - 4 Feb

POSITION	PLAYER TEAM	INDIVIDUAL		TEAM		TOTAL
		Plus	Minus	Plus	Minus	
Goalie						
Defence						
Defence						
Defence						
Defence						
Forward						
Forward						
Forward						
Forward						
Forward						
Forward						

FANTASY TEAM TOTAL

☆ BONUS BONANZA: Mega Manager | Footie Forecast ☒ | On the Ball ☒ |

WEEKLY FANTASY TOTAL

Result of Match ....

League Points awarded ....

League total so far ....

Top of the League this week .... points

Bottom of the League this week .... points

This week my team is .... in the League

ON THE BALL

The crowd is going wild! But can you spot the ball? You have just 30 seconds to find it and win a bonus point for your team for the week 5 Feb - 11 Feb.

SCORE CHART: 5 Feb – 11 Feb

POSITION	PLAYER	TEAM	INDIVIDUAL		TEAM		TOTAL
			Plus	Minus	Plus	Minus	
Goalie							
Defence							
Defence							
Defence							
Defence							
Forward							
Forward							
Forward							
Forward							
Forward							
Forward							

FANTASY TEAM TOTAL

☆ BONUS BONANZA: Mega Manager Footie Forecast ✕ On the Ball

WEEKLY FANTASY TOTAL

Result of Match ....

League Points awarded ....

League total so far ....

Top of the League this week .... points

Bottom of the League this week .... points

This week my team is .... in the League

SCORE CHART: 12 Feb - 18 Feb

POSITION	PLAYER	TEAM	INDIVIDUAL		TEAM		TOTAL
			Plus	Minus	Plus	Minus	
Goalie							
Defence							
Defence							
Defence							
Defence							
Forward							
Forward							
Forward							
Forward							
Forward							
Forward							

FANTASY TEAM TOTAL

☆ BONUS BONANZA: Mega Manager | Footie Forecast ✕ | On the Ball ✕

WEEKLY FANTASY TOTAL

Result of Match ....

League Points awarded ....

League total so far ....

Top of the League this week .... points

Bottom of the League this week .... points

This week my team is .... in the League

SCORE CHART: 19 Feb - 25 Feb

POSITION	PLAYER	TEAM	INDIVIDUAL		TEAM		TOTAL
			Plus	Minus	Plus	Minus	
Goalie							
Defence							
Defence							
Defence							
Defence							
Forward							
Forward							
Forward							
Forward							
Forward							
Forward							

FANTASY TEAM TOTAL

☆ BONUS BONANZA: Mega Manager | Footie Forecast ☒ | On the Ball ☒

WEEKLY FANTASY TOTAL

Result of Match ....

League Points awarded ....

League total so far ....

Top of the League this week .... points

Bottom of the League this week .... points

This week my team is .... in the League

SCORE CHART: 26 Feb - 3 Mar

POSITION	PLAYER	TEAM	INDIVIDUAL		TEAM		TOTAL
			Plus	Minus	Plus	Minus	
Goalie							
Defence							
Defence							
Defence							
Defence							
Forward							
Forward							
Forward							
Forward							
Forward							
Forward							

FANTASY TEAM TOTAL

☆ BONUS BONANZA: Mega Manager | Footie Forecast ☒ | On the Ball ☒

WEEKLY FANTASY TOTAL

Result of Match ....

League Points awarded ....

League total so far ....

Top of the League this week .... points

Bottom of the League this week .... points

This week my team is .... in the League

SCORE CHART: 4 Mar - 10 Mar

POSITION	PLAYER	TEAM	INDIVIDUAL		TEAM		TOTAL
			Plus	Minus	Plus	Minus	
Goalie							
Defence							
Defence							
Defence							
Defence							
Forward							
Forward							
Forward							
Forward							
Forward							
Forward							

FANTASY TEAM TOTAL

☆ BONUS BONANZA: Mega Manager   Footie Forecast ✕   On the Ball ✕

WEEKLY FANTASY TOTAL

Result of Match . . . .

League Points awarded . . . .

League total so far . . . .

Top of the League this week . . . . points

Bottom of the League this week . . . . points

This week my team is . . . . in the League

ON THE BALL

Here's a golden opportunity to score some points for your team. But only if you know a golden rule, or two! Get the right answers to both questions and add two extra points to your team's score for the week 11 Mar - 17 Mar.

1. PENALTY POSER!
The Cup Final has just begun —

Should be a cracking match!

Let's hope things liven up in extra time.

Oh well, you can't beat a good old penalty shoot-out...

Question: Which side takes the first penalty kick?

A. *The home team.*

B. *The team which won the toss.*

C. *The team which had possession of the ball when the final whistle went.*

2. Gordon the goalie, standing inside his penalty area, handles the ball outside the area. What penalty should Jeff give?

A. *Direct free kick.*

B. *Indirect free kick.*

C. *No penalty.*

I have scored _____ Bonus Bonanza points.

SCORE CHART: 11 Mar - 17 Mar

POSITION	PLAYER	TEAM	INDIVIDUAL		TEAM		TOTAL
			Plus	Minus	Plus	Minus	
Goalie							
Defence							
Defence							
Defence							
Defence							
Forward							
Forward							
Forward							
Forward							
Forward							
Forward							
			FANTASY TEAM TOTAL				
☆ BONUS BONANZA: Mega Manager			Footie Forecast ✕ On the Ball				
			WEEKLY FANTASY TOTAL				

Result of Match ....

League Points awarded ....

League total so far ....

Top of the League this week ....points

Bottom of the League this week ....points

This week my team is ....in the League

SCORE CHART: 18 Mar - 24 Mar

POSITION	PLAYER	TEAM	INDIVIDUAL		TEAM		TOTAL
			Plus	Minus	Plus	Minus	
Goalie							
Defence							
Defence							
Defence							
Defence							
Forward							
Forward							
Forward							
Forward							
Forward							
Forward							
			FANTASY TEAM TOTAL				
☆ BONUS BONANZA: Mega Manager			Footie Forecast ☒		On the Ball ☒		
			WEEKLY FANTASY TOTAL				

Result of Match . . . .

League Points awarded . . . .

League total so far . . . .

Top of the League this week . . . . points

Bottom of the League this week . . . . points

This week my team is . . . . in the League

SCORE CHART: 25 Mar - 31 Mar

POSITION	PLAYER	TEAM	INDIVIDUAL		TEAM		TOTAL
			Plus	Minus	Plus	Minus	
Goalie							
Defence							
Defence							
Defence							
Defence							
Forward							
Forward							
Forward							
Forward							
Forward							
Forward							
FANTASY TEAM TOTAL							
☆ BONUS BONANZA: Mega Manager			Footie Forecast ✕		On the Ball ✕		
WEEKLY FANTASY TOTAL							

Result of Match ....

League Points awarded ....

League total so far ....

Top of the League this week .... points

Bottom of the League this week .... points

This week my team is .... in the League

SCORE CHART: 1 Apr - 7 Apr

POSITION	PLAYER TEAM	INDIVIDUAL		TEAM		TOTAL
		Plus	Minus	Plus	Minus	
Goalie						
Defence						
Defence						
Defence						
Defence						
Forward						
Forward						
Forward						
Forward						
Forward						
Forward						
FANTASY TEAM TOTAL						
☆ BONUS BONANZA: Mega Manager		Footie Forecast ✕		On the Ball ✕		
WEEKLY FANTASY TOTAL						

Result of Match . . . .

League Points awarded . . . .

League total so far . . . .

Top of the League this week . . . . points

Bottom of the League this week . . . . points

This week my team is . . . . in the League

SCORE CHART: 8 Apr - 14 Apr

POSITION	PLAYER	TEAM	INDIVIDUAL		TEAM		TOTAL
			Plus	Minus	Plus	Minus	
Goalie							
Defence							
Defence							
Defence							
Defence							
Forward							
Forward							
Forward							
Forward							
Forward							
Forward							

FANTASY TEAM TOTAL	

☆ BONUS BONANZA: Mega Manager	Footie Forecast ✕	On the Ball ✕	

WEEKLY FANTASY TOTAL	

Result of Match . . . .

League Points awarded . . . .

League total so far . . . .

Top of the League this week . . . . points

Bottom of the League this week . . . . points

This week my team is . . . . in the League

SCORE CHART: 15 Apr -21 Apr

POSITION	PLAYER	TEAM	INDIVIDUAL		TEAM		TOTAL
			Plus	Minus	Plus	Minus	
Goalie							
Defence							
Defence							
Defence							
Defence							
Forward							
Forward							
Forward							
Forward							
Forward							
Forward							
					FANTASY TEAM TOTAL		
☆ BONUS BONANZA: Mega Manager			Footie Forecast	✗	On the Ball	✗	
					WEEKLY FANTASY TOTAL		

Result of Match . . . .

League Points awarded . . . .

League total so far . . . .

Top of the League this week . . . . points

Bottom of the League this week . . . . points

This week my team is . . . . in the League

ON THE BALL

Get ready for Jeff's final bonus blitz! The end of the season is approaching fast, so as a special treat he's giving you four chances to score bonus points for your team. What's more, in the week of April 22–28 you can give yourself up to three bonus points instead of two. Just this once though!

1. Mystery super star
Before becoming a sports commentator I was a footie super star – but do you know my name?
Claim one bonus point if you guess right!
- I hold the record for the most hat-tricks for England.
- I scored in my debut matches for Chelsea, Spurs, West Ham and England.
- I hold the record for the most goals in a single season for England.
- I was the First Division's top goal scorer six times between 1959 and 1969.

2. Buried treasure
And for one bonus point, which of the following is buried under Wembley Stadium?
A. A train.
B. A bus.
C. A car.

3. The world's most expensive player

Italy's Gianluigi Lentini was bought for a record sum by AC Milan in 1992. Guess correctly how much they paid for him and win a bonus point!

A. *£7 million*

B. *£10 million*

C. *£13 million*

4. Famous footballer

- I'm probably the most famous footballer in the world, but people don't use my real name. If you know what they call me, a bonus point is yours.
- I played for Brazil.
- Edson Arantes do Nascimento is my name.
- I helped my team to victory in two World Cups (1958 and 1970).
- In professional football, I scored 1,283 goals.

ANSWERS

1. Jimmy Greaves.

2. A train.

3. £13 million.

4. Pelé.

I have scored _____ Bonus Bonanza points.

SCORE CHART: 22 Apr - 28 Apr

POSITION	PLAYER	TEAM	INDIVIDUAL		TEAM		TOTAL
			Plus	Minus	Plus	Minus	
Goalie							
Defence							
Defence							
Defence							
Defence							
Forward							
Forward							
Forward							
Forward							
Forward							
Forward							

FANTASY TEAM TOTAL

☆ BONUS BONANZA: Mega Manager | Footie Forecast ✕ | On the Ball ✕

WEEKLY FANTASY TOTAL

Result of Match . . . .

League Points awarded . . . .

League total so far . . . .

Top of the League this week . . . . points

Bottom of the League this week . . . . points

This week my team is . . . . in the League

SCORE CHART: 29 April - 5 May

POSITION	PLAYER TEAM	INDIVIDUAL		TEAM		TOTAL
		Plus	Minus	Plus	Minus	
Goalie						
Defence						
Defence						
Defence						
Defence						
Forward						
Forward						
Forward						
Forward						
Forward						
Forward						
FANTASY TEAM TOTAL						
☆BONUS BONANZA: Mega Manager		Footie Forecast ☒		On the Ball ☒		
WEEKLY FANTASY TOTAL						

Result of Match . . . .

League Points awarded . . . .

League total so far . . . .

Top of the League this week . . . . points

Bottom of the League this week . . . . points

This week my team is . . . . in the League

THEY THINK IT'S ALL OVER – IT IS NOW!

League leaders or relegation rejects? It's time to see what your team's performance says about you.

FIRST PLACE – Congratulations!
The cup is yours! You've taken on the pick of the Premiership and won. Don't be surprised if Kenny Dalglish phones up, asking for tips – you're a magnificent manager!

2ND–5TH – Absolutely fabulous!
You certainly know how to pick a dream team. You must have the skills needed to be a top manager; motivation, footie know-how – and excellent dress sense!

6TH–9TH – Good effort.
If it hadn't been for that dodgy defender or muddled midfielder, this could have been your season. Give yourself a well-earned pat on the back.

10TH–13TH – Hmmm!

Look at it this way – at least none of your fans will ever die of excitement. Still, you've notched up a respectable result – and there's always next season!

14TH–17TH – Oooh err!

You've just managed to hang on by your fingertips. Seems your team lacked that certain something. Like the ability to score goals...

18TH–21ST – No comment...

First the bad news – if you finish here you've been relegated! Your team has joined the tired trio heading for the First Division. But there's good news as well – you can only do better in 1997!

LATE KICK-OFF QUIZ

Here's your chance to catch up on points for any weeks you may have missed. If you answer both questions correctly, you've won the match for that week and gain three League points. Get only one right and the match was a draw – that's one League point. If both your answers are wrong, your team was defeated for that week, giving you no points.

Answer both questions for each of the weeks you have missed and then fill in the results on the Score Charts.

14th August – 20th August

1. What do Coventry City supporters call their club?
   A. *The Sky Blues.*
   B. *The Red Devils.*
   C. *The Green Meanies.*

2.   Can a free kick be passed backwards?

My team has been awarded ___ points.

21st August – 27th August

1.   Which side plays at Ayresome Park?
  A. *Middlesborough.*
  B. *Aston Villa.*
  C. *Southampton*

2.   How many British teams were in the 1994 World
Cup finals?

My team has been awarded ___ points.

28th August – 3rd September

1.   How many League games did Jack Charlton
play for Leeds United?
  A. *534.*
  B. *629.*
  C. *687.*

2.   Which other London side has Wimbledon
captain Vinny Jones played for?

My team has been awarded ___ points.

4th September – 10th September

1. Scoring a goal against this side would mean getting the ball past players named Jakob, Erland and Dmitri. Which team?

2. Who is Wales' most capped player?
   A. Ian Rush.
   B. Neville Southall.
   C. Mark Hughes.

My team has been awarded ___ points.

11th September – 17th September

1. Which country scored the most goals in the 1994 World Cup finals?
   A. Sweden.
   B. Germany.
   C. Nigeria.

2. Which team did Gerry Francis manage before he moved to Tottenham Hotspur last season?

My team has been awarded ___ points.

18th September – 24th September

1. Where is the biggest football stadium in the world?

    A. *Italy.*

    B. *Uruguay.*

    C. *Brazil.*

2. Alan Shearer scored his 100th League goal last season. Who was it against?

Answers: 1. Brazil – the Maracaña Municipal Stadium can hold 205,000 people! 2. Chelsea.

My team has been awarded ___ points.

25th September – 1st October

1. Name the Premiership side whose previous grounds have included South Byker and Chillingham Road.

2. How much did Manchester United pay for Andy Cole last season?

    A. *£5.5 million.*

    B. *£7 million.*

    C. *£8 million.*

Answers: 1. Newcastle United. 2. £7 million.

My team has been awarded ___ points.

2nd October – 8th October

1. Which is the only club in the Football League to begin with the letter I?

2. Which club was originally called Belmont AFC?
   A. *Reading.*
   B. *Tranmere Rovers.*
   C. *Queens Park Rangers.*

My team has been awarded ___ points.

9th October – 15th October

1. Only four footballers have been knighted, the last one in 1994. Who was he?
   A. *Geoff Hurst.*
   B. *Jack Charlton.*
   C. *Bobby Charlton.*

2. Who plays at the Boleyn Ground, Upton Park?

My team has been awarded ___ points.

16th October – 22nd October

1. Which of these clubs has Manchester United captain, Steve Bruce, not played for?

A. *Norwich City.*
B. *Gillingham.*
C. *Leicester City.*

2. Gordon the Goalie grabs hold of the ball.
   How many steps can he take before he must put
   it back in play?

Answers: 1. Leicester City. 2. Four.

My team has been awarded ___ points.

23rd October – 29th October

1. Which club has been managed by Jimmy Hill,
   Terry Butcher and Don Howe?

2. How much did Blackburn Rovers pay
   Southampton for Tim Flowers?
   A. *£2 million.*
   B. *£3 million.*
   C. *£4 million.*

Answers: 1. Coventry City. 2. £2 million.

My team has been awarded ___ points.

30th October – 5th November

1. Who won the 1994 World Cup?

2.   And how many goals were scored in the final
        match?

My team has been awarded ___ points.

6th November – 12th November

1.   Which one of these footballing greats has not
        played for Tottenham Hotspur?
        A. *Peter Beardsley.*
        B. *Glenn Hoddle.*
        C. *Chris Waddle.*

2.   Which club did Chris Kiwomya play for before
        signing with Arsenal?

My team has been awarded ___ points.

13th November – 19th November

1.   Which Liverpool player appeared in every
        one of their League games in 1993–94?
        A. *Ian Rush.*
        B. *Robbie Fowler.*
        C. *Steve McManaman.*

2.   They've had home grounds at Clowes Street,
        Kirkmanshulme Cricket Ground and Pink

Bank Lane. Who are they?

A. *Bolton Wanderers.*

B. *Manchester City.*

C. *Crystal Palace.*

My team has been awarded ___ points.

20th November – 26th November

1. Who plays at Highbury?

2. Following a medical to investigate his headaches, which manager said, "At least it proves to everyone that I do have a brain!"?

A. *Terry Venables.*

B. *Jack Charlton.*

C. *Graham Taylor.*

My team has been awarded ___ points.

27th November – 3rd December

1. Which is the only other League side that Wolves hotshot Steve Bull has played for?

A. *Wimbledon.*

B. *Watford.*

C. *West Bromwich Albion.*

2. In the whole history of the club, which player has scored the most League goals for Manchester United?

My team has been awarded ___ points.

4th December – 10th December

1. Last season Manchester United had a spectacular 9–0 victory. Who were their unfortunate opponents?

2. And how many of those goals did Andy Cole score?

My team has been awarded ___ points.

11th December – 17th December

1. What is Bolton Wanderers' nickname?
   A. *The Stumblers.*
   B. *The Ramblers.*
   C. *The Trotters.*

2. Which side did Manchester City marvel Niall Quinn begin his League career with?
   A. *Tottenham Hotspur.*
   B. *West Ham United.*
   C. *Arsenal.*

Answers: 1. The Trotters. 2. Arsenal.

My team has been awarded ___ points.

18th December – 24th December

1. Wednesday wonder Des Walker played 264 games for his first club, Nottingham Forest. How many League goals did he score there?
   A. 0.
   B. 1.
   C. 3.

2. Which Scottish club is nicknamed the Jags?
   A. Falkirk.
   B. Partick Thistle.
   C. Kilmarnock.

Answers: 1. One. 2. Partick Thistle.

My team has been awarded ___ points.

25th December – 31st December

1. From which team did Tottenham Hotspur buy star striker Jürgen Klinsmann?
   A. Barcelona.
   B. Juventus.
   C. Monaco.

2. Who plays at Bramall Lane Ground?

My team has been awarded ___ points.

1st January – 7th January

1. Who did magical midfielder Andy Townsend play for before joining Aston Villa?
   A. *Liverpool.*
   B. *Sheffield United.*
   C. *Chelsea.*

2. Name the club known by its supporters as the Fiberts or the Foxes.

My team has been awarded ___ points.

8th January – 14th January

1. In the 1993–94 season, who was the only Everton player to be on the pitch for every League game?
   A. *Neville Southall.*
   B. *Tony Cottee.*
   C. *Paul Rideout.*

2. Does the ball have to be stationary when a player takes a free kick?

My team has been awarded ___ points.

15th January – 21st January

1. In the 1994 World Cup, who scored the goal in Ireland's awesome 1–0 victory against Italy?
   A. *Ray Houghton.*
   B. *Andy Townsend.*
   C. *Roy Keane.*

2. Which Premiership side is nicknamed the Dons?

My team has been awarded ___ points.

22nd January – 28th January

1. When Arsenal was founded in 1886, which famous team gave them their first strip and football?
   A. *Blackburn Rovers.*
   B. *Liverpool.*
   C. *Nottingham Forest.*

2. Who plays at Ewood Park?

My team has been awarded ___ points.

29th January – 4th February

1. Which of these sides has super striker Stan Collymore not played for?
   A. Crystal Palace.
   B. Southend United.
   C. Southampton.

2. In the Eighties, who was top of the League three seasons in a row?
   A. Liverpool.
   B. Manchester United.
   C. Everton.

My team has been awarded ___ points.

5th February – 11th February

1. Which Premiership side was Ron Atkinson managing at the beginning of last season?

2. And which side was he managing at the end of the season?

My team has been awarded ___ points.

12th February – 18th February

1. Who was the only Manchester United player to play in every one of their League games in the 1993–94 season?

   A. Peter Schmeichel.

   B. Denis Irwin.

   C. Ryan Giggs.

2. In the last Olympics which country won gold for football?

   A. Spain.

   B. Poland.

   C. Italy.

Answers: 1. Denis Irwin. 2. Spain.

My team has been awarded ___ points.

19th February – 25th February

1. "I think if they hadn't scored, we might have got a better result." Which Premiership manager made this classic comment?

   A. Alex Ferguson.

   B. Kevin Keegan.

   C. Howard Wilkinson.

2. Which London club plays at Stamford Bridge?

Answers: 1. Howard Wilkinson. 2. Chelsea.

My team has been awarded ____ points.

26th February – 3rd March

1. When were the first floodlights used at a British game?
   A. *1878.*
   B. *1908.*
   C. *1938.*

2. In the whole history of the club, who has scored the most League goals for Tottenham Hotspur?

Answers: 1. 1878. 2. Jimmy Greaves.

My team has been awarded ____ points.

4th March – 10th March

1. Which team was originally called St Jude's?
   A. *Wolverhampton Wanderers.*
   B. *Tranmere Rovers.*
   C. *Queens Park Rangers.*

2. Only two clubs in the Football League begin with the letter E. Name them.

Answers: 1. Queens Park Rangers. 2. Everton and Exeter City.

My team has been awarded ____ points.

11th March – 17th March

1. Can a penalty kick be passed backwards?

2. Apart from Liverpool, which is the only other club John Barnes has played for?
   A. *Reading.*
   B. *Middlesborough.*
   C. *Watford.*

My team has been awarded ___ points.

18th March – 24th March

1. Which club, formed in 1881, was originally called Stanley?!
   A. *Newcastle United.*
   B. *Bolton Wanderers.*
   C. *Sheffield Wednesday.*

2. Which club has been managed by Malcolm Allison, Terry Venables and Steve Coppell?
   A. *Manchester United.*
   B. *Norwich City.*
   C. *Crystal Palace.*

My team has been awarded ___ points.

25th March – 31st March

1. How many different countries have won the World Cup?
   A. Six.
   B. Eight.
   C. Ten.

2. Which team, two seasons ago, were star players, Chris Sutton, Efan Ekoku and Ruel Fox, all playing for?

My team has been awarded ___ points.

1st April – 7th April

1. Myrtle Road, Sheaf House and Olive Grove have all been called home by which Premiership side?
   A. Leeds United.
   B. Nottingham Forest.
   C. Sheffield Wednesday.

2. Which was the only country not to score a goal in the 1994 World Cup finals?

My team has been awarded ___ points.

8th April – 14th April

1. Which club is known by its fans as the Saints?
   A. Everton.
   B. Southampton.
   C. Newcastle United.

2. Which BBC commentator was Alex Ferguson talking about when he said: "If there's a prat in this world, he's the prat!"?
   A. Alan Hansen.
   B. John Motson.
   C. Jimmy Hill.

Answers: 1. Southampton. 2. Jimmy Hill.

My team has been awarded ___ points.

15th April –21st April

1. How many times has the World Cup final ended in a 0–0 draw?

2. Leeds United goalkeeper John Lukic also started his professional career with the Elland Road boys. Which other Premiership side has he played for?

Answers: 1. Just once – in 1994. 2. Arsenal.

My team has been awarded ___ points.

22nd April – 28th April

1. Match these clubs to the division they play in.
   A. *Stockport County.*   1. *First Division.*
   B. *Scunthorpe United.*   2. *Second Division.*
   C. *Stoke City.*   3. *Third Division.*

2. Which side, currently in the Premiership, has been managed by Tommy Docherty, Ron Saunders and Graham Taylor?

My team has been awarded ___ points.

29th April – 5th May

1. Which Premiership side's previous ground was called The Nest?

2. In England's final qualifying game for the 1994 World Cup, how quickly did opponents San Marino score?
   A. *9 seconds.*
   B. *19 seconds.*
   C. *29 seconds.*

My team has been awarded ___ points.